Natural Disasters

HURRICANES AND TORNADOES

Terry Jennings

Belitha Press

First published in Great Britain in 1999 by

Belitha Press
A member of **Chrysalis** Books plc
64 Brewery Road, London, N7 9NT

Paperback edition first published in 2003

Produced for Belitha Press Limited by Bender Richardson White
Project editor: Lionel Bender
Project production: Kim Richardson
Designer: Ben White
Text editor: Clare Oliver
Electronic make-up: Mike Weintroub
Illustrator: Rudi Vizi
Picture researchers: Cathy Stastny, Jane Martin & Daniela Marceddu
Consultant: Stephen Watts

ISBN 1 84138 047 4 (hb)
ISBN 1 84138 759 2 (pb)

Printed in Hong Kong.
10 9 8 7 6 5 4 3 2 1 (hb)
10 9 8 7 6 5 4 3 2 1 (pb)

British Library Cataloguing in Publication Data
CIP data for this book is available from the British Library

Photographic credits
Lionel Bender: 27b. **Alan Moller:** 1 & 17t, 21b. **Jim Reed:** 14, 15, 18t, 22, 25.
Gamma/Frank Spooner Pictures: 4t, 10t Richards, 19b D. Keister, 21 Miami Herald,
23t Weiner-Jones-Amberg, 28t: Today Florida. **Dr Joseph Golden:** 24b: NOAA.
Panos Pictures: 16 David Constantine, 20 Zed Nelson, 26 Caroline Penn, 28b Neil
Cooper. **Rex Features:** 23b. **Science Photo Library:** 7r John Mead, 10 NASA, 12
Sam Ogden, front cover and 17bl Fred K. Smith. **Terry Jennings:** 4b, back cover & 9.
Still Pictures: 7l Jorgen Schytte, 13 Julio Etchart, 27t Mark Edwards.

Words in **bold** appear in the glossary on pages 30 and 31.

Contents

Braithwaite
C.E.
Primary School

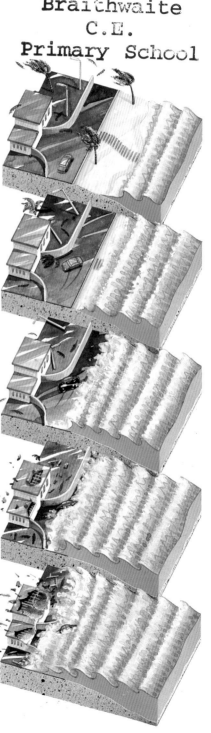

What are winds?

Sometimes the **wind** blows gently giving a refreshing **breeze**. At other times, a **gale** blows. People harness the power of the wind to turn windmills that pump water, grind corn or produce electricity. Yachts and sailing boats are powered by the wind, too. But the wind is not always useful. Sometimes it blows too strongly and whips up fierce **storms**, such as **hurricanes**. These damage houses, uproot trees and kill people.

▲ *A hurricane with winds topping 193 km/h hit southern England in October 1987. This toppled tree in London was among 15 million brought down by the storm.*

Moving air

Wind is air moving from one place to another. The air around the Earth is always moving. Air **currents** move from place to place because some parts of the Earth are warmed by the sun more than others.

When the sun warms the surface of the Earth, the air above is also warmed. As the air gets warmer it **expands** and so gets lighter. Because the warmer air is lighter than the surrounding air, it rises in the **atmosphere**, just like a hot-air balloon. Colder air from the surrounding areas then moves in to replace it. The wind blows because of the colder air moving in to replace the rising warmer air.

◄ *People have been using the power of the wind to drive windmills for thousands of years.*

Scale of strength

The first person to work out a way to measure the strength of the wind was Admiral Sir Francis Beaufort, in 1805. The **Beaufort Scale** was designed to allow sailors to guess the speed of the wind by looking at its effects on the ocean.

Looking at the wind

In this book we look at how strong winds are formed, how scientists study them and what effects they have on people, buildings and the land. This book also shows how people try to reduce storm damage.

▼ *The Beaufort Scale is used to describe wind strength. It has been adapted for use on land.*

Force 1
(2–5 km/h)
Light air

Force 2
(6–11 km/h)
Light breeze

Force 3
(12–19 km/h)
Gentle breeze

Force 4
(20–29 km/h)
Moderate breeze

Force 5
(30–39 km/h)
Fresh breeze

Force 6
(40–50 km/h)
Strong breeze

Force 7
(51–61 km/h)
Near gale

Force 8
(62–74 km/h)
Gale

Force 9
(75–87 km/h)
Strong gale

Force 10
(88–102 km/h)
Storm

Force 11
(103–120 km/h)
Violent storm

Force 12
(over 120 km/h)
Hurricane

Air power

The power of the wind can be useful as well as destructive. It can turn machinery or push along boats and ships. Before steam and diesel engines were invented, ships caught the wind in their sails to move themselves along. Small sailing boats are still used for fishing in many parts of the world. People also sail as a sport, or simply for pleasure, in yachts and dinghies.

Mills and pumps

In the past, people often used **wind power** to do heavy work. They built windmills that ground corn or pumped water. A windmill has large sails that are turned by the wind. Either the whole windmill or just the top and sails have to be turned in order to 'catch the wind'. The sails are fixed to a series of shafts and gear wheels. At the bottom of the vertical shaft is a heavy, flat millstone for grinding corn into flour, or a pump for draining water from the land.

Wind turbines

Today, large modern windmills, called **wind turbines** or wind **generators**, use the wind's energy to produce electricity. Wind turbines have blades that are like huge aeroplane propellers. The blades turn a shaft that is connected to an electrical generator.

▼ *Whatever the shape of the wind turbines' blades, they are designed to turn in the wind. Their turning action moves rotating rods, called shafts.*

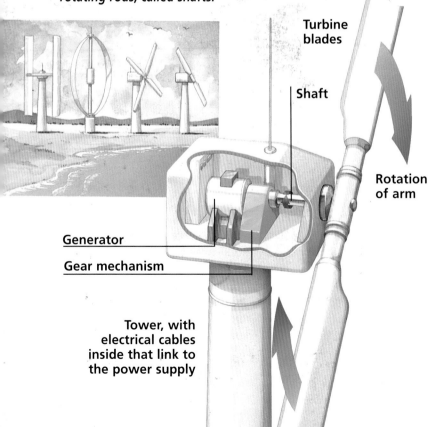

Turbine blades

Shaft

Rotation of arm

Generator

Gear mechanism

Tower, with electrical cables inside that link to the power supply

Endless energy

The larger wind turbines have an automatic control system that keeps the blades turned towards the wind. Unlike oil, coal or gas, the wind is one source of energy that will never run out – it is 'renewable' – and it does not pollute the air.

Pumping power

The wind is still used in many parts of the world for pumping water from wells and drainage ditches. Some wind pumps have fabric or slatted wooden sails.

▼ *At this wind farm in California, turbines produce electricity without polluting the air.*

Others are made by cutting an old oil drum in half and fixing the two parts to a vertical shaft. In Australia, America and parts of Europe, one common type of wind pump has a tall tower made of a steel framework. The rotating part has many steel blades and a large tail vane that turns it **windward**.

◄ *This simple windmill in Niamey, Niger, pumps up precious water from the ground.*

Winds of the world

▼ *How land and sea breezes are formed.*

SEA BREEZE BY DAY

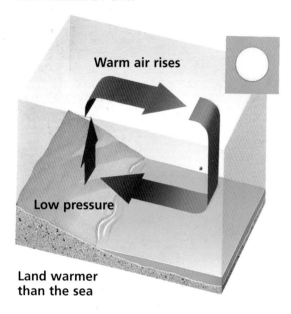

Warm air rises

Low pressure

Land warmer
than the sea

LAND BREEZE BY NIGHT

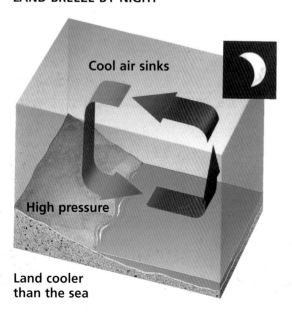

Cool air sinks

High pressure

Land cooler
than the sea

Very strong winds occur all over the world. But the most powerful winds, called hurricanes and **tornadoes**, are most common in hot places, such as the **tropics**.

Breezes

Winds often begin near the sea. Very light winds are called breezes. On a hot, sunny day on the coast, the land heats up more quickly than the sea. As the air is warmed it expands and so gets lighter and forms an area of low **air pressure**. The warm air rises and cooler air moves in from the sea to replace it; producing a sea breeze.

At night, the land cools down more quickly than the sea. Cold air sinks over the land and forms an area of high air pressure. The air over the sea is still warm, so it rises. The colder air moves in to take its place, producing a land breeze.

All winds start because the sun warms some parts of the Earth more than others. And winds always blow from areas of high air pressure to areas of low air pressure. The bigger the difference in pressure, the more forcefully the wind blows.

Special winds

Prevailing winds are the most common winds in a certain part of the world. There are three sets of prevailing winds each side of the **Equator**. If the Earth did not spin, these winds would blow roughly north to south. Instead, winds heading for the Equator are pushed westwards, and those blowing away from it are pushed eastwards. This is called the **Coriolis effect**.

Hot and cold winds

Winds that blow regularly often have names. The **trade winds** blow towards the tropics most of the year round. In the past, they were used by merchant sailing ships. In summer, the **monsoons** blow off the Indian Ocean in summer, bringing torrential rain to India, Pakistan and Bangladesh. In winter, they are cool, dry winds that blow from the land.

In southern France, a cold, northerly wind, the mistral, often blows for several days in March and April. By contrast, the Santa Ana is a warm, dry wind that blows through the mountains into California in the United States, sparking off bushfires on the way.

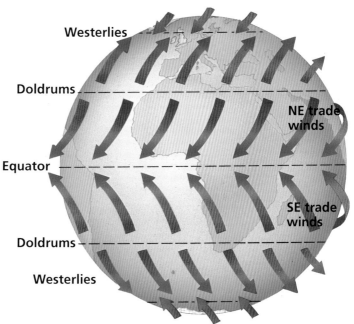

Polar easterlies

Westerlies

Doldrums

Equator

NE trade winds

SE trade winds

Doldrums

Westerlies

Polar easterlies

▲ *Prevailing winds blow because of the temperature difference between the Equator and the polar regions.*

▼ *This 'wind-pruned' hawthorn hedge in Norfolk, England, has been exposed year after year to prevailing winds that always blow in the same direction.*

Hurricanes

▲ *In September 1988, Hurricane Gilbert destroyed many parts of Jamaica, including its airfield. The storm lifted this aeroplane from the ground and dropped it into a tree.*

Certain winds are powerful enough to destroy whole towns. Such storms are called hurricanes in the Atlantic, but in the Indian and Pacific Oceans they are called **cyclones** and **typhoons**. They can blow at up to 350 km/h and bring torrential rain.

Birth of a hurricane

Hurricanes start to form in tropical **climates**, where the **temperature** is more than 27°C. **Weather** scientists believe that hurricanes form when the air is warmer than the surface of the ocean. Then they pick up vast amounts of energy and moisture as they rush towards the land. Only when the wind speed reaches 120 km/h is a storm called a hurricane.

▼ *This satellite image shows Hurricane Nora. Surrounding the eye are swirling storm clouds.*

Eye of the storm

A hurricane may measure 400 kilometres across. Inside it, the swirling mass of winds spiral upwards. At the centre or **eye** of the storm, the skies are clear and temperatures are high. The calm eye of the hurricane may be 40 kilometres across, but the strongest winds, with speeds of up to 350 km/h occur immediately around it. The storms with the smallest eyes are often the most powerful. Hurricane Gilbert, which occurred in 1988, was one of the most violent this century, yet its eye was only 13 kilometres wide.

Swirling clouds

Around the eye are thick, swirling **clouds** that tower 10 kilometres above sea level. As this warm, moist air spirals upwards and cools, the **water vapour** cools and turns to rain and the hurricane's energy is released. It takes several days for a hurricane to travel from the ocean where it was born to the land. The average life of a hurricane is a week or two. Although warnings are given during this time, it is difficult to tell exactly in which direction a hurricane will travel.

Hurricane names

Clement Wragge (1852–1922), an Australian **meteorologist**, was the first person to think of giving hurricanes names. He chose names of people from the Bible, such as Rakem, Sacar and Talman. Later, the United States Weather Bureau gave only female names to hurricanes. Since 1978, they have drawn up a list of alternate boy's and girl's names, in alphabetical order. Each time a new hurricane is detected by meteorologists, it is given the next name on the list.

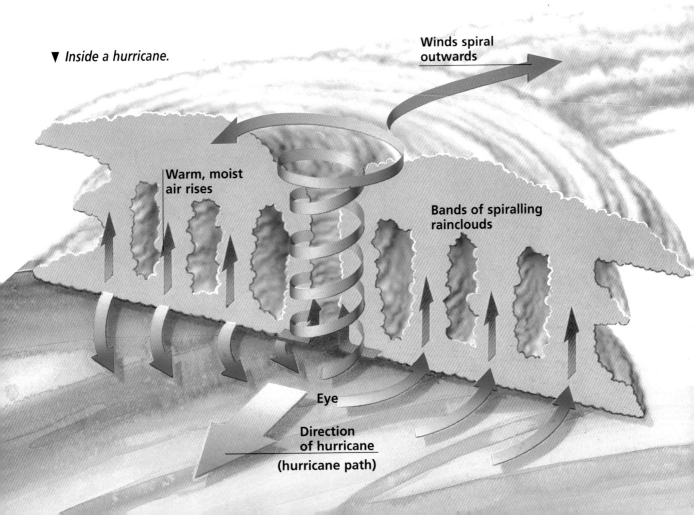

▼ *Inside a hurricane.*

Winds spiral outwards

Warm, moist air rises

Bands of spiralling rainclouds

Eye

Direction of hurricane (hurricane path)

Hurricane damage

Just one hurricane can unleash more energy in a single day than 500 000 atomic bombs. Its winds uproot trees. Boats are lifted from harbours, flung over sea walls and smashed to splinters far inland. Houses are destroyed as their roofs are torn off, while large lorries are lifted off the road. Electricity cables and telephone wires are ripped from their poles. Anyone who is caught outside stands little chance of survival.

Giant waves

Worse still, the force of the hurricane pushes up huge **waves** on the sea. The water level near or under a hurricane can be 5 metres or more higher than that of the calmer seas around. These waves are called a hurricane **surge**. When the waves reach land, they cause serious **floods**.

▼ *Hurricane Bob hit the east coast of the United States on 19 August 1991. This yacht in Massachusetts was tossed to shore like a toy.*

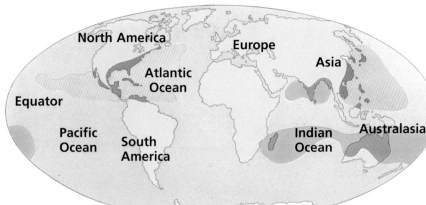

◄ This map shows the areas of the world where hurricanes are most likely to occur.

Areas with up to five hurricanes a year

Areas with more than five hurricanes a year

▼ Hurricane Mitch devastated Honduras in 1998. When the storm had passed, there was a lot of clearing up to do. It will take many years to rebuild the buildings, roads and people's lives.

A hurricane surge

A hurricane surge may last only a few hours, but its crashing waves usually cause severe damage. Nine out of ten deaths in a hurricane are from drowning.

Hurricane Mitch

Hurricane Mitch struck Central America in 1998. By the time Mitch reached land it had wind speeds of 280 km/h. The full force of the hurricane surge hit two of the poorest countries in the world, Nicaragua and Honduras. To make matters worse, a year's rain fell on the area in the same week. Over a million homes were washed away. Roads collapsed, crops were destroyed, and bridges and power lines were swept away. Parts of the Honduran capital city were buried under 12 metres of mud and water.

The fury abates

Hurricane damage occurs mainly on islands and in coastal areas. The storm usually dies out fairly quickly once it is away from the ocean. This is because it takes its energy and moisture from the sea.

Studying hurricanes

▲ *Hurricane researchers stop their Doppler radar truck on the road to study a severe storm.*

Finding out more about how hurricanes form could make it possible to prevent them, or at least to reduce the damage they cause. But hurricanes are very difficult to study. They destroy scientific instruments and kill anyone who gets too near them.

Inside a hurricane

A few, specially-strengthened aeroplanes can fly through a hurricane. Their crews have reported that the heaviest rain seems to fall in spiral bands.

The water vapour inside the clouds instantly turns to ice on the plane's wings. Inside the eye, the air is pure and clear, while the surrounding clouds rise up in tiers, like seats in a theatre. There is a dome of blue sky far above the hurricane.

Other aeroplanes, called hurricane-hunters, fly around the edges of these storms. Onboard, they have special **radar** equipment, which is accurate enough to monitor the speed of a single raindrop. These planes track the position and direction of storms.

Satellites

Satellites take pictures of storms as they grow. These images help scientists to predict when a hurricane is going to develop, and what its likely path will be. Other satellites have special sensors that record changes in the temperature of the ocean surface as a hurricane forms in the atmosphere. Most importantly of all, satellites keep track of every small low pressure area that might lead to a full-blown hurricane. In this way, advance warning of a hurricane can be given.

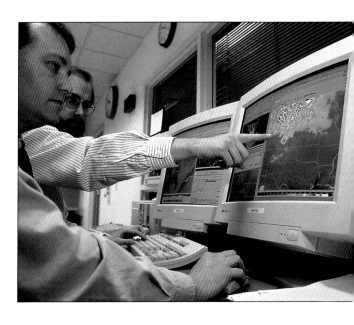

▲ *To learn more about storms, meteorologists study images showing how past storms behaved.*

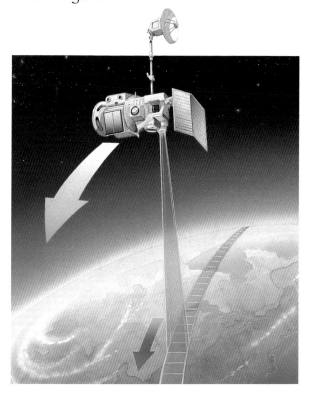

▲ *The Landsat satellite constantly circles the Earth, photographing and monitoring cloud patterns and the ground, section by section.*

'Seeding' hurricanes

Some American scientists tried to reduce the power of hurricanes before they could cause serious damage. They dropped tiny crystals of salt, ice or silver iodide into the clouds from planes. The idea was that moisture would gather around the crystals that they had planted and produce droplets big enough to fall as rain. This would increase the size of the hurricane's eye and weaken the storm.

The winds did drop, but picked up again almost at once. The storms also changed course and went on to hit places that might otherwise not have been affected. The project was abandoned.

Tornadoes

Tornadoes are small, extremely powerful **whirlwinds** that form very suddenly. The word tornado comes from a Latin word meaning to twist or turn. In fact, in the United States tornadoes are often called twisters.

Tornado groups

A tornado is quite different from a hurricane. It is smaller, faster and more violent. Tornadoes often occur in small groups and, unlike hurricanes, they are most common far inland. A tornado is a violent, rapidly-twisting funnel of cloud that stretches down from a storm cloud to the Earth's surface. It travels across the land at speeds of only 30 to 65 km/h. But the highest wind speeds on Earth occur inside a tornado, with speeds sometimes topping 800 km/h. A tornado may measure anything from just a few metres to more than 100 metres across. It can travel for more than 200 kilometres before it uses up all its energy.

▼ *A house and car have been destroyed, and a boat overturned, by a tornado that hit Joliet, in Illinois, in the United States.*

Where tornadoes occur

Tornadoes are most common and most violent in the United States. On average, about 1000 tornadoes occur there every year. But tornadoes also happen regularly in parts of Canada, Argentina, China, Australia, Southwest Asia and even Europe. The United Kingdom has between 15 and 30 small tornadoes each year.

A tornado destroys everything in its path. It sucks up dust, sand, cars, buildings, even people and animals. It eventually dumps these things when it dies out.

▲ *A tornado, such as this one in Texas, in the United States, sucks up anything in its path, rather like a giant vacuum cleaner. It looks black because of the dust and dirt which it sucks up.*

▼ *Double trouble: alongside this waterspout on Lake Okeechobee in Florida, in the United States, a large bolt of lightning shoots down from the storm cloud to the water.*

Waterspouts

If a tornado forms over a lake or the sea it is called a **waterspout**. When its funnel touches the surface of the water, it sucks up tiny droplets of water. These colour the waterspout white.

Waterspouts usually last between ten minutes and half an hour. Although they are less powerful than land tornadoes, some waterspouts have picked up and wrecked boats and jetties. If they reach land, they destroy buildings, too. In January 1998, a waterspout at Selsey in southern England damaged more than 1000 houses before it returned to the sea.

How twisters form

Cumulonimbus cloud

Rotating column of air

Direction of the tornado

Thunderclouds are the birthplace of tornadoes. Warm, moist air cools as it rises and its moisture forms dense, towering thunderclouds. The proper name for these is **cumulonimbus clouds**. Strong winds develop as cold air rushes in to replace the rising air. If the rushing air begins to rotate, a tornado forms.

Thunderclouds

Even in places where tornadoes are most common, very few cumulonimbus clouds produce tornadoes. They usually produce heavy rain, thunder or hail.

A danger sign is when dark patches of cloud, shaped like stubby fingers, hang from the base of the thundercloud. These may grow, until a funnel-shaped cloud hangs down for a little way below the parent thundercloud. Even at this stage, many funnels fade away after about ten minutes or so. But sometimes the funnel keeps on growing. The cloud twists downwards faster and faster, until the funnel reaches the ground.

◄ *As a tornado moves over the ground, it picks up anything in its path, including buildings, vehicles and trees.*

◄ *Radar studies showed that a tornado was about to develop from this 'wall cloud' over farmland in the United States.*

At first the tornado, like all clouds, is made up only of tiny water droplets. But the second that the cloud touches the ground, it starts to suck up soil, dust and other debris. That is why a tornado soon appears almost black.

Tornado times

Although forecasters can predict the days when tornadoes are likely to occur, they still do not know enough to say exactly when and where they will hit. In the United States, tornadoes have been known to strike in every month. What the

forecasters can say for sure is that tornadoes are more likely in summer, especially in May and June, when the air is warmest and wettest. For the same reason, they are most likely to happen in the late afternoon and least likely to form at night, when the air is cooler.

► *All tornadoes form at the base of a thundercloud, but only a few thunderclouds give rise to tornadoes. On rare occasions, a tornado with twin funnels develops.*

Tornado destruction

▲ In Bangladesh, children study in a temporary outdoor classroom. Their school building was destroyed by a tornado.

Although a tornado affects only a small area, it can be more destructive than any other kind of weather.

Wind speeds

It is impossible to measure wind speeds inside a tornado because it destroys the recording equipment, but they usually top 480 km/h and sometimes exceed 800 km/h. Buildings, trees and crops are completely destroyed, although the track of the damage is rarely more than a few hundred metres wide.

Under pressure

A tornado creates sudden changes in air pressure and these cause most of the damage. At the centre of the tornado, the air pressure is very low. The pressure inside the houses on the ground remains normal. As the whirlwind passes over, the sudden drop in outside air pressure causes the air inside the house to expand violently. As a result, the house explodes like a burst balloon.

Flying fridges

The debris caught up in the tornado can be flung at fantastic speeds. People are stripped of their clothing, sheep are shorn of their wool and chickens lose their feathers. Asphalt may be sucked up from the surface of the roads, and bark flies from the trunks of trees.

Pieces of straw are fired like darts into tree trunks. Trains have been lifted and dropped back on to the track facing the other way. Fridges have been carried 200 kilometres. Lighter debris, such as paper, can be scattered up to 320 kilometres away.

▲ *May 1997: a tornado passes over Miami, Florida, in the United States. Skyscrapers such as these are built to sway – rather than snap – in strong winds.*

Severe tornadoes

A whole swarm of tornadoes struck the Madaripur district in Bangladesh in April 1977. Almost 900 people were killed and more than 6000 injured. Bangladesh was also the scene of the world's worst tornado disaster, in 1989, in which 1300 people died.

In May 1999 a series of tornadoes swept across Oklahoma and Kansas, USA, in a region called Tornado Alley. There were two major tornadoes and up to 74 smaller ones. The winds killed at least 45 people and thousands of people were left homeless.

► *In Texas, in the United States, an apartment building and its surroundings have been destroyed by a tornado. Two people were killed, and several badly injured, in this disaster.*

Strange rains

Once a tornado loses its energy, the objects it has picked up come crashing down to earth. That is why, from time to time, some very peculiar things rain down from the sky.

Flying lorries

In May 1990 in the United States, for example, a tractor and trailer got caught up in a twister. The tractor was picked up and then dropped about 115 metres away without bouncing at all. The trailer, which was loaded with scrap metal, ended up in a field about 330 metres from the road, having bounced five times along the way.

In 1982, in the town of Bicester, Oxfordshire, England, a man saw a tornado lift a lorry trailer over a 2-metre-high fence. Surprisingly, the fence was undamaged.

Lucky escapes

Still more frightening was the experience of a young Chinese girl who lived near Shanghai. In 1992 she was sucked up by a tornado and carried almost 3 kilometres before she was set down, unhurt – in the top of a tree!

▲ *When a twister hit Harristown, Illinois, United States in April 1996, it lifted cars into the air then smashed them to the ground. It also ripped the roofs from houses.*

When a tornado swept across Arkansas in the United States in 1995, a baby boy was sucked from his cot as his home was destroyed. The boy was later found in a ditch about a kilometre away. He was muddy, but had only a few scratches and bruises. Elsewhere in the United States, a whole school was swept up by a tornado and dumped 137 metres away. The building was destroyed, but all 85 children inside survived the flight.

Raining rats and frogs

Throughout history there have been stories of showers of fishes, frogs, rats, lizards or other animals falling down from the sky. Many of these stories are made up, but some could be real-life experiences resulting from tornadoes.

In 1932, a nine-year-old girl living on a farm in England was out walking when a storm broke. Mixed in with the rain were tiny frogs. The girl's dog went berserk and nearby cows stampeded in fright. The terrified girl ran home and told her parents what had happened, but they never believed her story.

In East London in 1984, people found fish scattered over their back yards and gardens. It seems a waterspout on the River Thames had sucked the fish up into a cloud and carried them some distance before dropping them.

▲ *In Charlestown, South Carolina, United States, a tornado lifted boats from their moorings and dropped them in the middle of the street.*

Even stranger, when a tornado struck a farm in Nottinghamshire in England in August 1997, a hut containing 40 pigs was sucked into the air. The farmer watched in amazement as the hut swirled around 30 metres above his head. Eventually, the squealing pigs were shaken out on to nearby roofs.

◄ *Sheets of corrugated iron were ripped from roofs and thrown into the air by a tornado that struck the city of Darwin in Australia.*

Tracking tornadoes

Tornadoes are very difficult to predict. They occur so often in the Midwest of the United States that it is known as Tornado Alley. But even in Tornado Alley, only one per cent of all thunderclouds give rise to a tornado.

Radar tracking

Since 1977, a special kind of radar, called Doppler radar, has increased the accuracy of tornado forecasts. Doppler radar detects the circular movements inside a storm that develop into tornadoes. The radar can predict a twister about 25 minutes before it emerges from the base of the clouds. This gives just enough time to send out warnings.

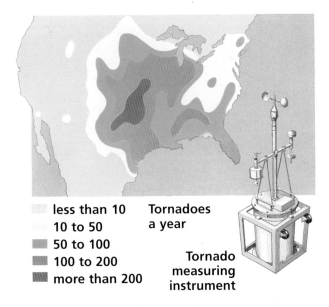

less than 10
10 to 50
50 to 100
100 to 200
more than 200

Tornadoes a year

Tornado measuring instrument

▲ On this map of the United States, areas in different colours show tornado hot spots, including Tornado Alley in the Midwest.

Scientific research

Scientists at Oklahoma in the United States are studying tornadoes by using planes to drop instruments in and around them. They also use trucks that have weather stations fixed to their roofs. These collect the measurements made by high-altitude weather balloons that are flown right into the centre of tornadoes.

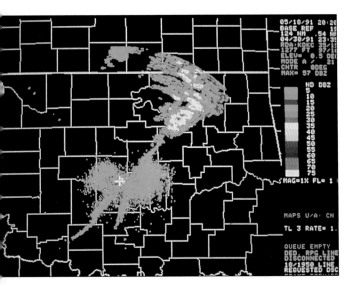

◄ Doppler radar is used to map the tornado's path. This radar screen image shows a tornado passing over Oklahoma in the United States.

▲ *'Storm chasers' photograph and video the build up of tornado conditions.*

Other trucks carry specially-strengthened instruments. These are strong enough to withstand the full force of a tornado. They are placed on the ground to measure the changes in temperature and air pressure as the tornado passes over them.

Storm chasers

Being a tornado scientist can be a dangerous job, but some of the people who live in and around Tornado Alley put themselves in even greater danger. These twister enthusiasts are called 'tornado chasers'. Their hobby is to follow the paths of tornadoes by car, plotting the storm's progress on a map. Chasers often give advance warnings to towns that there is a tornado on its way.

Satellite snaps

As with hurricanes, the warning signs of tornadoes can be picked out in satellite photographs. One sign that a tornado is about to develop is when a swelling appears above a thundercloud. Another typical sign of a tornado is when a group of circular clouds join to form a long, curved wall that ends in a hook-shape.

Clouds of dust

When there is much less rain than usual for the time of the year, we say there is a drought. Drought can happen in places that normally receive a heavy rainfall, not just in hot, desert areas.

Dust storms

One effect of drought is **dust storms**. These happen when high winds sweep up loose dirt and sand from the ground and swirl it about. A dust storm can be up to 640 kilometres wide, and lift the dust to heights of 4300 metres. It can shift millions of tonnes of material in a few hours. Dust from the Sahara has even been blown to the British Isles and parts of South America.

▼ *A villager walks through a dust storm near his home in Dodoma, Tanzania.*

Choking dust and lost farms

During a dust storm, you cannot see more than 400 metres ahead. The air is so thick with dust that it suffocates any living thing. The dust and sand piles up in heaps, some more than 4 metres high, that block roads and railways. Windows are sandblasted into sheets of frosted glass, and paintwork is worn away. Even after the winds drop, the dust may stay suspended in the air for days. It filters the sun's rays and creates beautiful sunsets. But dust storms also remove valuable soil from farmland. Each year, farmers in the United States lose 20 million tonnes of soil to dust storms and in Russia, 400 000 hectares of farmland are ruined.

▲ *Left unprotected, tonnes of valuable soil can be blown away in dry, windy conditions. Hedges and belts of trees shelter the soil and stop the dust storms from forming.*

Dust devils

Dust devils, or whirlwinds, are spirals of spinning air, like small tornadoes. The dust devil's rotating funnel is created when hot ground heats the air above it. But these gentle, fair-weather whirlwinds usually do not last very long or cause serious damage.

Dust devils are very common in the hot, dry desert and semi-desert regions of Africa. They form in **temperate regions** sometimes, too, over ploughed fields on hot, summer days.

◄ *Dust devils form in hot, dry parts of the world, such as here in southern Morocco.*

Wind defences

▲ *These caravans in Florida in the United States were blown over by a tornado that struck in February 1998.*

Strong buildings offer some protection from most kinds of wind damage. Caravans, mobile homes, holiday chalets and flimsy wooden buildings are usually among the first to be damaged in strong winds. Wooden or metal shutters can be closed over windows to reduce the dangers from flying shards of glass.

Building regulations

In the United States, strict building laws ensure that properties built near the coast are constructed to withstand the force of storm surges created by tornadoes. New houses are placed well back from the shore and are built on raised land.

Better forecasting

Scientists are getting better at forecasting when and where violent tornadoes and hurricanes will occur. This is saving lives. For example, tornadoes killed about 100 people in the United States each year during the 1970s. By the 1990s, the number was 50.

◄ *Concrete shelters, such as this one in Bangladesh, protect people from hurricane surges.*

Loud and clear

In the United States, radar and volunteers are used to keep watch for tornadoes. If a twister is spotted, a warning is broadcast and sirens may be sounded. This gives people a small amount of time to shelter in a special storm cellar, a strong building or in a central room of their own home, away from windows and outside doors. There they are protected by internal walls.

Racing tornadoes

Trying to escape a tornado in a car is extremely dangerous. A tornado travels too fast and its track is too unpredictable for drivers to be able to avoid it. When a tornado with winds of 320 km/h neared Wichita Falls in Texas, United States, in 1979, some people jumped into their cars and tried to race it. However, these drivers accounted for 26 out of the 43 people who were killed, and 30 out of the 59 people who were seriously injured. Most of the victims' homes were undamaged.

Hurricane scale

Each hurricane is given a number from one to five. It helps when deciding whether to board up windows, seek the safety of a storm shelter or to evacuate the area, to know how strong the hurricane will be. Category 5 hurricanes are the most feared. Hurricane Mitch, which caused terrible damage and many deaths in Central America in autumn 1998, was a Category 5 hurricane. Fortunately, such hurricanes hardly ever happen.

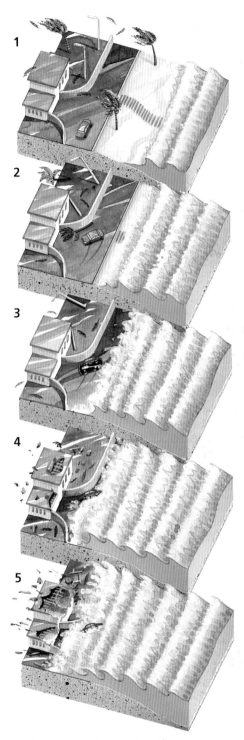

▲ The higher the number the hurricane is given, the greater the damage it is likely to cause. Category 1 hurricanes cause minimal damage. Category 4 and 5 hurricanes cause extreme to catastrophic damage.

Glossary

air pressure The weight of the Earth's atmosphere pressing down on the surface.

atmosphere The thick layer of air that surrounds the Earth. Above the atmosphere there is no more air, only space.

Beaufort Scale A scale used to measure the strength of the wind.

breeze A wind you can just feel.

climate The average weather of a region of the Earth throughout the year.

cloud A patch of tiny water droplets which we see floating in the sky.

Coriolis effect Describes how winds tend to follow a curved path because of the Earth's rotation. In the northern hemisphere, this curve is to the right; in the southern hemisphere, it is to the left.

cumulonimbus cloud A large, billowing flat-topped cloud that soars up into the sky.

current The movement of air or water in a particular direction.

cyclone Another name for a hurricane or typhoon.

dust storm A strong wind which sweeps along large quantities of dust and sand.

Equator The imaginary line around the middle of the Earth.

expand To become larger.

eye A fairly calm, clear area at the centre of a hurricane.

flood A flood occurs when water spills over on to the land from a river, a lake or the sea.

gale A strong wind that breaks twigs off trees and is very hard to walk against.

generator A machine that produces electricity when it is turned. Also called a dynamo.

hurricane A powerful, swirling storm found in tropical parts of the Atlantic Ocean. Such storms are called cyclones or typhoons in Asia and willy-willies in Australia.

meteorologist A scientist who studies the weather.

monsoon A wind that brings heavy rain. The strongest blows from the Indian Ocean in summer, bringing rains to southern Asia.

prevailing wind A wind that almost always blows from the same direction.

radar A system of bouncing radio waves off an object and timing their return to work out how far away the object is.

satellite Something that moves around something larger. The Earth, for example, is a satellite of the sun. Man-made satellites orbit the Earth collecting information about the weather.

storm A period of violent weather. Storms usually have strong winds, dark clouds and heavy rain, snow or hail.

surge A sudden rush of water.

temperate regions The lands that lie above the Tropic of Cancer and below the Tropic of Capricorn. Here, the climate is cooler than in the tropics and milder than at the north and south poles.

temperature The measure of how hot or cold something is.

tornado A very violent whirlwind. A tornado is also called a twister.

trade wind A tropical wind blowing towards the Equator, either from the north east in the northern hemisphere or from the south east in the southern hemisphere.

tropics The regions near the Equator that have a hot climate all the year round. They lie between the Tropic of Cancer in the north and the Tropic of Capricorn in the south.

typhoon Another name for a cyclone or hurricane.

waterspout A tornado over the sea.

water vapour The gas or mist that forms from water when water is heated.

wave A regular movement of the surface of water caused by the wind.

weather How hot or cold, or wet or dry the air is at a particular time.

whirlwind A very strong wind that whirls around or blows in a spiral.

wind Air moving from place to place.

wind power The use of moving air to produce electricity or to push along boats, ships and other vehicles.

wind turbine A large, modern windmill, with blades like aeroplane propellers, that is used to produce electricity.

windward Facing the oncoming wind.

Index